DEATH
AND
TRANSFIGURATION

Also by Kelly Cherry

Poetry

God's Loud Hand
Natural Theology
Relativity: A Point of View
Lovers and Agnostics

Nonfiction

Writing the World
The Exiled Heart

Fiction

My Life and Dr. Joyce Brothers
The Lost Traveller's Dream
In the Wink of an Eye
Augusta Played
Sick and Full of Burning

Limited Editions

Time Out of Mind, *poetry*
Benjamin John, *poetry*
Songs for a Soviet Composer, *poetry*
Conversion, *fiction*

Translation

Octavia, *in* Seneca: The Tragedies, Volume II

DEATH
AND
TRANSFIGURATION

POEMS

KELLY
CHERRY

LOUISIANA STATE UNIVERSITY PRESS

BATON ROUGE AND LONDON

1997

Designer: Melanie O'Quinn Samaha
Typeface: Futura and galliard
Printer and binder: Thomson Shore, Inc.

Library of Congress Cataloging-in-Publication Data
Cherry, Kelly.
    Death and transfiguration : poems / Kelly Cherry.
        p.   cm.
    ISBN 0-8071-2211-4 (cloth : alk. paper). —ISBN 0-8071-2212-2
(pbk. : alk. paper)
        I. Title.
PS3553.H357D4   1997
811'.54—dc21   97-14754
                                                                  CIP

Very grateful acknowledgment is made to the following publications, in whose pages some of these poems first appeared, sometimes in slightly different form or under different titles: *The American Scholar:* "Remembering"; *Calapooya Collage:* "Dove of Light"; *Columbia: A Magazine of Poetry & Prose:* "Alzheimer's," "Bubbling"; *Christianity and Literature:* "I Went to Find You"; *Crosscurrents:* "Anniversary"; *Denver Quarterly:* "Hide-and-Seek"; *Hellas:* "How We Are Taken"; *Isthmus:* "The Almost-Baby"; *Kentucky Poetry Review:* "From Venice: Letter to an Ex-Husband" (as "Letter to an Ex-Lover"); *Lilt:* "Kissing in the Silver Summer House Above the Black Sea," "Yalta Rain"; *The Lullwater Review:* "At a Resort by the Black Sea"; *The Madison Review:* "Miracle and Mystery"; *Ms.:* "My Mother's Stroke"; *The Nebraska Review:* "Regrets"; *The New Orleans Review:* "Wind Chimes in the Deep Blue Upside-Down Heaven"; *The New Virginia Review:* "What You Do Now"; *Other Poetry* (England): "The Dead Vole" (as "The Dead Mouse"); *Prairie Schooner:* "Epithalamium," "Imagining the Past" (as "The Other Side of Time"); *The Southern Review:* "As If a Star," "Emphysema," "The Letter," "My Mother's Swans," "On Fire and Living on Air" (as "One Remorseful Last Day"); *Tar River Poetry:* "Petition on Behalf of My Parents (Both of Whom Had Emphysema)," "Trip to Las Vegas."

"Bedroom with Yellow Lamp and Chrysanthemums" first appeared in the chapbook *Time Out of Mind* (March Street Press, 1994). "My Mother's Swans" and "My Mother's Stroke" were reprinted in Sanders, ed., *The Decade Dance: A Celebration of Poems* (Sandhills Press, 1991). "My Mother's Stroke" was also reprinted in Mukand, ed., *Articulations: Poetry About Illness and the Body* (University of Iowa Press, 1994) and in Pettit, ed., *The Writing Path 2* (University of Iowa Press, 1996). "Alzheimer's," "How We Are Taken," and "The Almost-Baby" were reprinted in *The Writing Path 2.* "Alzheimer's" was also reprinted in Ray and Ray, eds., *Fathers: A Collection of Poems* (St. Martin's Press, 1997).

In appreciative acknowledgment of their recognition and support (both sustaining), I wish to thank the Fellowship of Southern Writers, the Hawthornden Foundation, the Corporation of Yaddo, the Virginia Center for the Creative Arts, the Wisconsin Art Board, and the University of Wisconsin.

Thanks also to the abiding spirits of Michael Pinkston (1953–1995), whose kindness and encouragement are a lasting legacy to all the authors with whom he worked, and my beloved dog, Duncan (1979–1996).

CONTENTS

II

J. Milton Cherry, 1908–1986

Mary Spooner Cherry, 1912–1988

Jonathan Silver, 1937–1992

I

In the darkened room children were crying.

—Anna Akhmatova, "Requiem"

IMAGINING THE PAST

More difficult than imagining the unknown
Is imagining what once you knew,
Boardwalk and Park Avenue,
The pick-up sticks, each the palpable equivalent of a single tick
Of the clock
That long, malaiseful hour before Sunday dinner.

In Finland, a woman said to me,
Whatever you lost will come back to you
If it belonged to you.
She had lost her brother, her father, her mother
In Leningrad during the Great Patriotic War.

In that same city, Leningrad,
I last saw the man I always thought
I would marry.
Once upon a time,
I played the piano.
Once upon another time,
I memorized the *Iliad* and lulled myself to sleep at night
Silently reciting its rhythms to myself.
He had a Bechstein; he knew Chinese.

When I lived in the hospital for crazy people,
I wrote poetry at night in the psychiatrist's empty office.
A man, not a psychiatrist, said to me, not in the hospital,
I can promise you one thing: no matter how hard you try
To kill yourself,
Someday you will have to die.

Who, now, can imagine playing the piano,
Having forgotten how to play the piano?
Do you know Greek?

Do you know your brother, or even your lover?
Can you imagine not who you might have been but who you were?
And the man and woman who played pick-up sticks with you,
While the roast was basting—
Where are they,
Those kindhearted grown-ups?

Her mother is going away now,
Perhaps to Leningrad, perhaps to the other side of time,
Taking with her all that the child knew
Of music and poetry
And Sunday afternoons as impatient as childish sighs.
Her mother is ascending, is flying
Upward to light, like Haydn's lark.

A shadow falling everywhere now. That we must live forever
In the subsequent hush of our parents' banishment
From earth.

MY MOTHER'S SWANS

They are crystal and gold,
Prismatic and opaque,
Gliding across the gentle lake
Of her memory as if called
Forth or deeply compelled

By that music—that deceptively delicate
Music with its urgent undertow
Dark as love that lays us low,
Pulls us down where its weight
Bursts our eardrums like water's weight—

That is its own spindrift, eddy and wake.
When did my dear mother grow old?
I think it may have happened when she was still a child,
Sunburnt, sleepy and dream-laden, listening to her south-flying-swans' wings
    playing the lake
Like a violin, or later, when, for my father's sake,

She came indoors, took off her outlandish, inflated water-wings,
And put away all childish things—
But not quite. In Richmond,
She smiled as she bought me a feathery white swanlike cloche, and in London,
A wind-up swan that sings

That shadowy theme. Her own swans drift
Across the windowsill in a spill of light. They are not wild;
They do not stop at Coole, nor do they light on the lake she knew as a child
Or even the lake of her mind. They move continuously, like music, that dan-
    gerous, irresistible rift
We navigate between rest and rest, art's brave launch and final, balletic lift—

The transcendent, escaping craft.

MY MOTHER'S STROKE

Your right eye goes blank,
Can't see even the dark.
The dog barks, and you hear
No bark.

Messages your brain sends
Down your left side, derailed,
Never get where they're going,
And the slow slide

Of your whole brain
Is like that of that train
To Southend—
Went straight off at the bend, didn't it,

And into the lake.
But you can still make
The odd, small gesture,
That thought-out investiture

Of movement with sense,
And in your mind, you dance
Under the lake. The puff-fish, the pancake,
Even the devilfish trailing his whispery wake

Nod and bow
As you waltz underwater.
The music bubbles to the surface and me,
Your wondering, admiring, loving, listening daughter.

WIND CHIMES IN THE DEEP BLUE UPSIDE–DOWN HEAVEN

In this poem, God is a fish
And light floods the cove like high tide.
A rainbow swims in the sea.
I am safe on high ground, holding
The hand of my small daughter.

I am not safe. I have no daughter.
I am my mother's daughter
And I am holding her hand,
But she is drowning.

We have left the poem. I have let go
My mother's hand, and it is my fault that
She is drowning. Now no one can save her
Except God, who is a fish with scales like wind chimes.
In the deep blue upside-down heaven, God glows as if phosphorescent.

On his silvery back, my mother rides
Away from me, grasping his fins in her hands.
All the music I have ever known is becoming fainter and fainter,
Ebbing into silence.

In the poem, the name of the daughter I do not have is Rainbow,
And I am holding her hand because she must never leave me,
But I am drowning because I have no daughter,
And the light that poured out of the sky has drained into darkness
Earlier than anyone expected.

THE LETTER

She goes to Wales. Sits on a rock, facing the sea.
O Mother, what do you see?
What mast, what flag, what ship's sails?

All light has been leached from the rain,
Which is as dull as chronic pain.
O Mother, are you all right?

You write of such loneliness
As we can only guess
At. Mother, are you all right?

The ocean dies under its weight of water.
I am your killing daughter.
I fear your stillness, you who were perpetually, brilliantly, in motion,

And the undeclared ship approaching from the west, darkness staining the sky
Like something permanent: indelibly.
O Mother, that rough water is so blackly deep!

EMPHYSEMA

My mother writes that my father is mute.
His voice has drowned in his throat.

It has fallen asleep in the cave of his chest,
Little dreaming beast.

It swings in his throat from a rafter
Of flesh, hanging laughter.

(Her gallows humor.) He cannot speak,
Who so seldom spoke. Say he makes timid mouse-squeaks,

Gasps for air like a fish on a beach:
He is leaving us for a new world beyond our reach,

Silent and airless, where music is inward, and the starlings strung
On the sky like notes on a staff won't sing but are sung

By the evening wind,
The evening wind.

MIRACLE AND MYSTERY

Miracle and mystery
      Are swans mated
For the whole of history,
      Their pairing fated.

The bread we cast upon the waters
      Is what they live on.
They are not martyrs,
      Though they dive down

And down, through dark green depths, to find
      Love in the lake.
Their movement ripples the mind.
      They love each other for our sake.

If one dies, the other grieves
      Itself to death.
Two lives,
      One breath.

EPITHALAMIUM

For my parents' Golden Anniversary, 1983

Although he is still surprised
That it has turned out this way
After all the years when
It seemed it wouldn't,

My father loves my mother
So much that there are times when
He is afraid he is going to die
Of it, the anxiety,

And there are times when
He thinks that would be a relief,
Better than the dis-ease of heart
That awaits him when she goes.

With his arthritic fingers
He threads the needle
She can no longer see
The eye of.

ANNIVERSARY

A man and a woman lie down
together, and when they get up,
they leave the imprint of their love
in that place, and it is a kind

of fossil, invisible to
all but the trained eye. The trained eye
spots the fossil and reconstructs
the past, as if a symphony

were to be unraveled from a
single note. The trees of the time
reappear, ringed with light, and the
cardinal returns for a bow.

Encore, encore. Even the man
and the woman return, white-haired
now, complaining of aches and pains,
and they wonder if they need new

glasses, as they take in, first, their
surroundings and then realize
each other's presence, the last man
or woman they had expected

ever to find themselves with, here
at the end of so long a time.

ALZHEIMER'S

He stands at the door, a crazy old man
Back from the hospital, his mind rattling
Like the suitcase, swinging from his hand,
That contains shaving cream, a piggy bank,
A book he sometimes pretends to read,
His clothes. On the brick wall beside him
Roses and columbine slug it out for space, claw the mortar.
The sun is shining, as it does late in the afternoon
In England, after rain.
Sun hardens the house, reifies it,
Strikes the iron grillwork like a smithy
And sparks fly off, burning in the bushes—
The rosebushes—
While the white wood trim defines solidity in space.
This is his house. He remembers it as his,
Remembers the walkway he built between the front room
And the garage, the rhododendron he planted in back,
The car he used to drive. He remembers himself,
A younger man, in a tweed hat, a man who loved
Music. There is no time for that now. No time for music,
The peculiar screeching of strings, the luxurious
Fiddling with emotion.
Other things have become more urgent.
Other matters are now of greater import, have more
Consequence, must be attended to. The first
Thing he must do, now that he is home, is decide who
This woman is, this old, white-haired woman
Standing here in the doorway,
Welcoming him in.

PRAYER FOR MY FATHER: IN MEMORIAM

After reading Portraits and Elegies *by Gjertrud Schnackenberg, in which the poet mourns her dead father*

Now that you're gone I find you everywhere:
In poems by strangers, even in the tercets
My students write, art their hopeful prayer.

Yes, you—so single-minded you seemed to care
About your violin more than life's best bets—
Are gone. And now I find you everywhere:

At night, by day, even in a sudden air
Game-showed during the interval of the Saturday Met's
Live broadcast ("Mozart!" is one contestant's prayer).

And yet, I think you were not ever there,
Or else why was I calling, calling? Death lets
Us draw close, and now I see you everywhere—

Omnipresent, like God, both far and near—
And in my mind, you play the late quartets.
To my students who write, for whom art is prayer,

Explain that this is art: seeing what is here
Or not here, hearing music made of notes like old debts.
You are gone, but now I find you everywhere
In all I write, poetry my prayer.

BUBBLING

They call it *bubbling*—
saliva rising in the dark pond of the mouth
like a small but insistent tide,
a desire to escape, perhaps,
before death drags even this upwardly mobile element down
to the caverns and abysses
sluggishly irrigated by the Styx's unseen tributaries, before
the soul's slippery passage
away.
     The minute I see it
I know you are going, you are
giving up or in and nothing
I can do will call you back.
I ring for a nurse, pressing the buzzer
twice to let them know that this time
it's different, this time they are being summoned
to my mother's death.
              "Bubbling?"
I ask the Pakistani.
She has her arms folded atop her stomach which is softly mounded
like a basket full of laundry, and
though I know she is kind she is
also cynical, and the way her eyebrows
fly together over her clothespin nose makes her look
angry.
     She nods. It slows,
now, this phenomenon—just one more
bodily process, one more
manifestation of how we are
dependent on the material.
My mother is trying to breathe but
only her mouth moves and then
not even that and I

give up, give in to tears,
the insistent tide of them
pushing out from behind my eyes.

PETITION ON BEHALF OF MY PARENTS
(BOTH OF WHOM HAD EMPHYSEMA)

Both gone. They have been burnt to bone,
Then ash, then smoke.
Two as one. Now none.

I think of them as air—
The very thing they could not get enough of.
Oh! In exactly the same way—I think of them as love,

Love invisible but everywhere.
Therefore, let them breathe love
Like air.

Let it fill their souls
Until they ascend, higher and higher,
Gone with the fire,

The eternal wind.

HOW WE ARE TAKEN

Lines written while thinking of my recently deceased parents and what they are missing

How deeply we are taken by the world
And all its glories—how it draws us in,
Until we are surrounded by the pearled
Light of late day, the cool transparent rosin
Of a clear sky across which the virtuoso
Sun (this image reminds me of my father)
Has swiftly drawn its fine Italian bow,
Espressivo. And breathe—and smell—the rather
Romantic, yet classical air. And feel it too—
This world's beauty present to all our senses,
Surprising them, like guests who jump out at you
From behind chairs and couches, or like sentences
That draw you in and take you where you never
Expected to go and wish you could live forever.

QUARTET WITHOUT BEGINNING OR END

Perhaps they play their violins in some
place where the strings are never out of tune
and never break. Haydn and Beethoven come
in and take seats; never again, the jejune
Debussy! From here on—for eternity—
they'll play only the real stuff, which survives.
As *they* do, on that South Bank of the City
of God, where music is the soul of That Which lives
forever, quartet without beginning or end.
Musicians' lives go on inside the music,
a shadow-score, and though the melody's darkened
by pain, transposed to the key of sorrow by sickness,
it's brightened by the brilliance of violins,
for there is music even in such silence.

FALLING

The air fills up with ghosts—
mother, father,
even dead movie stars (so far past their prime
they're willing to audition, for the role of a lifetime).
And they are like stars,
if also like shadows at night,
a concentration of space,
crumpling of light,
fiery and not quite invisible
(though invisible)
billiard balls of bright spirit
rolling overhead,
underfoot,
until you are afraid to move,
you might step on them they might
trip you up send you falling
down the stairs you
clumsy thing you,
arms and legs all in a scrawl
like handwriting on a wall.

BEDROOM WITH YELLOW LAMP AND CHRYSANTHEMUMS

They sleep here—the ghosts,
Their otherworldly dreams shimmering in still air,
Their steps on the stair
As light as the heavenly host's

Would be, if angels had feet,
But not so bright—a certain blueness haunts the house,
Hangs in the closet with clothes,
Shades the windows facing the street.

Silently, silently, they love each other,
Those bodiless waves of light, kissing nothing.
Love is a purgatorial flight from everything
Through memory, a return to the lost father-mother

Who chastens us in our beds.
Submit, submit. The darkening angels crowd
Around you like a gathering cloud.
Day ends in night.
And this daughter never weds.

FROM VENICE: LETTER TO AN EX–HUSBAND

(*The Horses of San Marco*)

I am riding on bronze,
Astride a sea-city.
I love my horse
With more than human pity.

His helpless eye,
His cool, wide flank
Are no less real than yours,
I frankly think.

His deep gold hue is like liquid,
As if a canal had been poured into the mold
Of a horse. He canters
Above the world,

Bold as the sky,
Eternity between his teeth
Like a bit.
Oh I love my

Horse with more than human
Love, with love
That is truer, animalistic,
Given to no man.

On him I ride
Through salt air and
The sinister, traitorous streets,
Sculpture's bride.

ON LOOKING AT AN ARTWORK BY MY EX–HUSBAND, AFTER HIS DEATH

Such precise measurements of anguish!
The proportionate modeling of protest and despair!
This sculptor welds thought
to air,
finds a material form for the cast of his mind.
But I remember you in bed
next to me, young, your angry words hammering my heart
as though you mistook it for stone. How invisible and unsaid,
forever, that body I slept next to, arm like an armature
beneath my neck, our dreams a hairbreadth
apart. . . . I loved you then and now,
despite that pain, this pain, death.

THE FIGHT

I think, sometimes, of how you used to rage,
remember words you hurled at me like sticks
and stones—or like grenades. An explosion like sex,
at first, and later on, a cold dark rampage
that laid waste to the quiet country of my heart.
For days on end, I might as well have been
missing in action in a small Southeast Asian
territory. And you the lover of art,
of rationality! The pacifist!
Oh, you the one who never was missing or lost!
I held my hand in front of my then-young face
to keep away those words—that acid, that mace—
and still you seized my wrists and pulled me to you
to kiss or kill me. Which, I never knew.

AS IF A STAR

And if—and if—? Would *that* have been enough
for you? I think you always looked for more—
more anything. More *everything*. More of
whatever it was that not having all of it tore
you up. . . .
                    You in the living room, lights off,
with Schoenberg or Shostakovich on
the record player (that long ago); the cough
of cigarette; anger—or desperation,
perhaps it was that—as dark as the darkened room.
And I was timid, I was wanting too,
wanting something, something . . . oh, the bride her groom.

The record stopped. The silence surrounding you
            then was extraordinary. As if you were a star,
            owning the space around you, and burning, and far.

FIRST MARRIAGE

I held you, or I never held you, or I held you briefly, once, long ago, and you kissed me while my heart kept time.

Or perhaps not, perhaps it was your heart beating, so hard I mistook it for my own.

But surely the paint was new in the floor-through in the Brooklyn brownstone. And I know there was music.

White walls. Books everywhere . . .

And I remember how the still rooms filled with sun.

You may have taken me into your arms as the music (something by Schoenberg, all twelve tones as sweetly reserved and mysterious as a sundial), beginning in a place of peril and possibility, found its way home.

You may have loved me.

Or perhaps not, perhaps it was my heart beating like a metronome.

To touch—to be. To be within the compass
Of another! . . . But life, or art? And if it's life
You want, how will you make it good, a passing
Grade (be moral person and loving wife)?
And if it's art—you know the problems there,
You know enough to know how it will go:
Your mind on fire, and you living on air.
One day you'll die without having seen the show.
The clouds will drop out of the sky like ducks
Shot down. The trees will keel over silently.
You'll lie in bed, wishing that you had fucked
When there was time for it, gently or violently.
The clouds move closer, smothering and gray.
It's going to be one remorseful last day.

REGRETS

YOUNG WOMAN

They are what she intends to have none of.
Other people may grow old and bitter
But she is sure that she can do better
Than that, when it comes to work and even to love.
You have to live in such a way as to
Stay free of forces that would make you feel
You are a failure, or someone whose soul
Has been torn or singed or anyhow knocked askew
By the horrible knowledge that there still are left
So many thrilling things you meant to do.
She holds her drink aloft, this gesture a cue
For someone to applaud the marvelous gift—
A pearl of her wisdom. In the glass, the olive
Shines like a sort of pearl. *Oh*, she says, *live!*

OLDER WOMAN

I thought that that was what I was doing.
Not throwing time away, not failing to make
The best use even of tragedy and heartache—
For these, I saw, were the things that I had going
For me (as they go for us all). I was determined
To outsmart time not by outrunning it
But by devising a way of turning it
Into a past that would never be out of mind.
Regrets are sneaky—the way they sneak up behind
When you aren't looking and then you have to turn
Around, like Orpheus, and this is how you learn
What you have lost and never again can find,
Your younger self, who dared to see, in an *olive*,
A simile, and such sober reasons to live.

HIDE–AND–SEEK

The children have fled
Into the musk-scented twilight.
Their faces are wavering
In gray light
That were as safe and sure
As the white markers
In the swimming pool
That separate the shallow
From the deep.
The children have fled.
Our lawn is bare of children.
Oh tell us, please, where have the children fled?
Into the musk-scented twilight,
Their pointy elbows and knees
Bouncing like badminton birds
Erratically through the night.
Those of us left on the verandah
May sip brandy or vermouth,
Replenishing our tans with mosquito repellent.
Looking at one another, we will ask,
Where have the children fled?
Are those their faces,
Wavering there,
In dying light?

THE ALMOST–BABY

It was an almost baby,
Inadvertent tissue
Unexpected
At this late date,

A mere mouse
Of a baby.
We set no bait gates—
They were unnecessary.

The baby dropped down the flue
Of my body, dead
As a sparrow.
I love you more than bone loves marrow.

I love you more than God loves sorrow.
Tomorrow
I'll eat toast and think
About you, the way

You slept on top of me,
Your lips at my breast,
Me smiling, glad and knowing
That my cup was overflowing.

I love you more than
The almost-baby,
More than my populous blood, the well-schooled fish
Egging each other on

In their ovarian currents,
Diving for air.
I love you more than life
Or death, my dear.

THE DEAD VOLE

Like a baby's sock lost on the path.
Thing in which only the smallest foot might fit.

And the river rushing by, as if to get somewhere—
A harem of midges kissing the air in a frenzy of love—
The wind shoving leaves aside, on a tear—

But this stays, unmoving.
Thin tail a dropped thread,
A thought someone had and forgot.

Hands and feet perfectly formed
And as sweet as a newborn child's.

The curl of body like a lock of hair.

Poor little vole,
Brown leaf
Fallen
In summer,

With your face turned away,
Down,
As if what you saw
Is even now not for us to see.

TWO LIEDER FOR LOST CHILDREN

I

The apple blossoms shimmer in late snow—
a seen music,
a fragrant song.

The petals drop.
The music darkens into blood.

II

And who would they have been?
More than shadows, more than birthday wishes.
Men and women, every one more original than sin.
Such bright lights, quick as flashes!

Then wish and shadow again.

TRIP TO LAS VEGAS

Blackjack, roulette.
I play the casino coquette

Though I'm forty-three, too old.
I shall wear the bottoms of my blue jeans rolled.

Darling, I'm a good bet
Because what you see is what you get,

If you can just be happy with what you get.

But can you? Can you?
You say you want a change of venue?

You say you want someone
With a more winning way?

Someone new with whom to play?

I'm here with you because I thought
I had finally hit the jackpot—

Love. But no such luck.

WHAT YOU DO NOW

You take lessons: driving, swimming.
You change the color of your hair
From blonde to brown or brown to blonde.
You take a Frequent Flyer trip to someplace where

Life is different: L.A.
Or the Yucatán,
Say. You acquire a tan.

In L.A., the houses cost half-a-mil
And smack of tacky.
You think the natives are wacky

Or maybe you are, stretched out on a gurney like a corpse
While Sophia waxes your legs.
You start to keep charts, counting your eggs

As they exit monthly. Your stock's
Running low.
Go

Elsewhere, try sky-diving, study Minoan
Architecture. You've got time.
You've got time. You've got time.
You could go redhead, turn yourself out in some smart rhyme.

AT A RESORT BY THE BLACK SEA

They are building a tennis court by the Black Sea.
Guests will raise a racket—or two or three.
Meanwhile, the workmen hammer away,
And the sun sails over the Crimean mountains
Like a ball served by an unseen god
Over the net of the horizon, and it lands in the center of the court
Of a disappearing Russia, love's last resort.

KISSING IN THE SILVER SUMMER HOUSE ABOVE THE BLACK SEA

The sea at the base of the mountains was black, a black-olive sea, and the sky so clear we could look through it to *the world unseen*, and the sweet salt air like a letter mailed from September to August, bearing news of the coming autumn, when I last saw you, in the year before the Revolution, in the silver summer house, that small pavilion with shining pillars we leaned against, kissing.

YALTA RAIN

How gently the rain fell,
    as if careful not to bruise the earth.

And the mountains were like blue flames
        that continued to burn,
    though it rained.

    All day I thought of you,
   what lives we might have led
had history not intervened
    in biography.

    Even the rain fell along straighter lines
than those our lives have followed!

Now we are falling, slowly,
  in spirals,
    spiraling down to earth.

    Let us fall gently.
        Let us hurt nothing,
   not even a leaf.

REMEMBERING

In the ruining garden,
In the closed house,
In the dwindling light
And rain, always rain,
I think of you again

And the grass sweetens,
The house brightens,
Night wraps itself around
My shoulders, a shawl
Woven of the darkness of the fall

But warm and dry,
And stars appear
In the sky, like burning kisses
Blown by the solar wind—
Here, from a time out of mind.

I WENT TO FIND YOU

As in a dream, I heard you call my name
And went to find you, but you were not there.
A shadow on the snow was blue as flame,
Blue as water, blue as the cold night air,
And in this blueness you were hidden but crying
My name, a word whispered among dark leaves
So that it seemed as if the sky were sighing.
It's true: with you gone, even the sky grieves.
This is to say love burns, but at a distance
Like a star. Or like a blizzard of stars.
Or like snowflakes falling like stars in a dance
Of twisting and turning, blown to blue. Or like tears.
And when I heard you call my name and went
To find you, I found that I had merely dreamt.

DOVE OF LIGHT

A dove of light spreads bright wings in blue air over the Crimean mountains
and takes flight, resting first on this birch branch, now on that pine bough,
and at last at home, folds them, as if in prayer,
as if in night.

LIVADIYA PALACE, SITE OF THE YALTA CONFERENCE

Here and here and here,
They sat and signed.
You take that country, why don't you.
We'll keep this one, if you don't mind.

And nobody minded.

The Black Sea was blue.
Salt air burned in the bright sun
Like sea salt in a Georgian stew.

And flags flew.

Sick, old, mad,
They sat and signed.

Who knew,
Who, then, knew. . . .

The flags flew.
Dinner was fine,
Followed by brandy
And port wine.

A DIMINISHING CHORD MODULATING INTO NIHILISM

On a certain day the bombs appeared, like hailstones,
in the sky, massive yet brisk, their falling
creating a kind of music, a diminishing chord
modulating into nihilism and the silence that is sound's
inescapable shadow. This music was so tormentingly sad
one could barely stand to hear it. Dogs and donkeys pretended to hear nothing,

as did people, and for a time, it seemed even no *thing*
would acknowledge the vibrations of these new rolling stones.
Yet all the while the bombs were falling, we were feeling, though inexpressibly,
    sad.
We felt as if our own bodies, still upright, were falling
into themselves, collapsing without sound
into an absence of light, like burnt-out stars, of their own accord.

Given this situation, respect must be accorded
all of us who so calmly accepted that nothing
would alter the situation at that point, nothing would reinvent sound
as an art capable of opposing sadness. Angels do not, these days, roll back
    stones
from sepulchers, nor could they, in fact, convert what was, from the sky, falling
into anything that might rise. This dearth of resurrections is sad,

but true. (Theologians, who stubbornly celebrate it, nevertheless have sad
faces and are like Christmas packages wrapped in bright paper with dull brown
    cord.)
Therefore, when the bombs began their carefully orchestrated falling
from the sky, they were as perfectly rehearsed as anything
that ever existed, as everything that exists on earth—apples, sparrows, hail-
    stones—
falls, sooner or later, and often without making a sound,

but on this day, there was a kind of sound,
and it was a sound like the absence of light, which is to say, a sound so sad
even the animals outside the barn banged their heads against the stone
paddock, praying for deafness. We heard chords
never heard before—they were like nothing
in the history of music or the world, these notes falling

from the sky with the bombs falling from the sky, our bodies falling
like scree from a cliff. It was both a merciless and a philharmonic sound,
and the cadenza of its silence lasted until nothing
else lasted. The trusting dogs and innocent donkeys, deeply and unendurably
    saddened,
folded themselves in small places and died listening to those chords
that rang through the cold air as the bombs struck the earth, a kind of stoning.

Fallen like prideful angels, we asked, finally, if we ourselves were really any
    different from, say, Muammar Qaddafi or Saddam Hussein
    . . . or anyone else dying to be known. (Something we should have known.)
We sounded one another out, devised Treaties and Accords,
but it was too late. In time, the bombs became their own echoes. *And then
    nothing, not even one sweet, last tone.*

THE REVELATION AT HAND

A century closes—guilty twentieth
Of twenty Yeats described—but nothing returns.
There is nothing that will repeat itself
As a pattern on the pane through which we gaze
These days at dark rain falling on a facing
Of red rock, where rooks caw. Nothing comes back
To be born again. Our horrors are ever new—
Or else, I think, they are the same horrors
They always were, unchanged, continuous.
The rain blackens the brick chimney, like soot,
Or as if blood could burn to ash, and in smoke
And black rain one reads only contamination,
The slow leakage of scientific empires,
A wasting like Chernobyl, an unconcern.

No child now teaches us, to make us parents
Of a new philosophy, or enacts innocence,
That we might recover that drowned country
From the blood-tide. Nor, in desert sands, stirs
There some meaning, amid winged, turning shadows,
Which, though we must fail to comprehend
Its monstrous fullness, reveals anything at all,
Except its lion body, human head.

II

Labour is blossoming or dancing where
The body is not bruised to pleasure soul,
Nor beauty born out of its own despair. . . .

—W. B. Yeats, "Among School Children"

REQUIEM

ONE: ABSOLUTE ARGUMENTS

All absolute arguments can be argued both ways.
      For example, if someone draws an equivalence
Between his own sufferings and those of victims of the Holocaust,
      There can be no morality,
And if he does not draw an equivalence between his own sufferings
      And those of Holocaust victims,
There can be no morality.

And yet there can be no argument that does not also take into account
      The cardinal that is a small cataract of blood,
The rain falling between branches
      As if weaving itself on the loom of the winter tree,
My memory of you,
      And this: that the knowledge we will die is not forgotten
But not impossible to live with—

A beautiful bird like blood,
      Spilling itself carelessly out of the sky.

I sometimes think there's no such thing, really, as self-pity,
      Since for the sufferer the world does not exist.
(If the world doesn't exist, neither does the self—
      Only the suffering.)
If so, those who attempt to shake someone out of it
      Are mistaken in their approach to the problem,
And what is required is not an argument

But a way to remake the world.
      For example. It was a time, for me, of sadness.
Of endless, paralyzed afternoons deep as secret pools
      That dropped off steeply into night.

—A sadness sharply defined
        By the recent deaths of my parents.

I cannot deny that I awaited both deaths as a liberation
        From various sentences pronounced
Long ago. One is filled
        In spite of oneself with anticipation.

But nothing turns out as expected,
        And in any case, anticipation
Is not all one is filled with.
        Everyone else who used to live there, in that house,
Including the dog,
        Has died.
Nor is all sadness as repetitive and compulsive as a mirror.

I thought that if there were ghosts
        The way they would render themselves invisible
Would be by appearing in forms we thought we knew—
        Mourning doves, or the trembling aspens,
The Norwegian spruce, the pitch pines
        Pining for whatever it was their changed souls had loved
When they were alive as humans. . . .

True suffering obliterates the world.
        To feel sorrow for others is therefore a form of happiness;
To feel sorrow for others is to have been blessed.
        Blessed are those who grieve,
For they shall feel sorrow for others,

As I did, thinking of you in a foreign city,
        Tanks ranked at the barricades.
Or: As I did, watching my mother leave her body,

And I wanted to call her back
But she was already too far away to hear me,
        Or for me to hear her.
And you didn't make a sound.

You were always self-effacing, a considerate man,
        Wanting not to ask for more than you had a right to,

But from the beginning you knew that there could be no argument
        That did not take into account the cardinal,
As red as a Marxist text,
        And the intricately woven rain,
And my memory of you, which is as absolute
        As both sadness and happiness.
How is it possible to remake the world?

It has been lost, it has spilled itself
        Carelessly out of history,
And how is it possible for us to re-create it?

Is there no God
        Willing to act twice?

I believe
        That if there is a God
It is a God that reveals itself
        As it comes to know itself,
Eternally revealed and eternally unknown.

It is a power and presence
        That must be exactly congruent
With our consciousness of it
        And yet greater, for

The idea is always a projection of the reality and
        If the reality is human consciousness
God must be an idea

Both greater than human consciousness and mapped by it.
        In a poem, Red Warren writes of "consciousness"
That "loses faith in itself." I mean to speak
        Of consciousness discovering its manifest destiny,
Its belief in itself
        As a fact,
And one that must push us ever onward

Into consequence. Perhaps I don't know how to put this
        Precisely, but perhaps I will. I am trying to know
Things that stay just outside the window
        Of language, and yet the romance of ambiguity
Has never appealed to me, not even when
        My hands trembled,
I was too excited to hold still,

Merely because a man I loved—you,
        In that city—
Had decided to love me back.
        Now rain stitches these black branches with silver.
Yes, and the cardinal is most certainly like a line by Christopher Marlowe,

And I am trying to say
        What I believe, for I believe it is time.
Time to take a stand, and to know where one stands.
        Our parents have disappeared
During the night, wandering aimless with Alzheimer's
        Or kidnapped by one disaster or another, or—if only this!—off on a
            lark forever,

And we are alone, here
        In this haunted, shuddering house, wind
Rising and falling like broken chords outside the window.
        They were so careless, to go away
Like that. . . . Not even a good-bye . . .
        I do not believe that there is a God
That will rescue them or bring them back.

I do not believe in a God
        That can keep those whom we have loved
Safe from life or death.
        I believe that we are so extremely mortal
(And so unprotected)
        That only a God greater than that which I can conceive
Could do that,

But I believe that there is a divinity
        Within us that we kill, and kill again,
And yet it rises, baffled, sad, and loving,
        Returning like the sun,
And we kill it once more,
        And it goes down into death
To be born.

TWO: "BEAUTY BORN OUT OF ITS OWN DESPAIR"

It was never a child—only a wavelet of blood
        Spilling itself carelessly out of my body—
But I thought of it as a child,
        Or perhaps a very small god,
Something like a miracle, if not actually a miracle
        (Since it died and did not come back,
In any form).

Meanwhile, there were events everywhere—
        Weather, marriages, layoffs.
Anything could happen, but did it matter,
        And if so, to whom?
And what were we going to make of it?
        Under the streetlamps,
The tanks crouched like animals
        Ready to spring.

I wondered whether someone would steal my mother's wedding ring.
        She had asked to have it burned with her.
It was cheap—worn to a thinness, like herself,
        But it was a ring, it was gold, why
Waste what wouldn't be missed—

I decided it didn't matter—

I left that house, that lawn
        Where all the trees seemed to be weeping
All the time, and when I locked the door
        Behind me,
I felt as if the past had shut me out.
        The past has no use for us,
Yet—

I returned to America,
        Making that old journey again.

Events are everywhere.

In the corridor a girl was screaming.
        Nurses dragged her to an empty room,
Left her bound and drugged,
        Her blonde bangs in her eyes,

She needed a haircut,
          She needed someone to love her,
She thought she needed to die.

I think about this, about that girl,
          And I don't know what to do.
It is as if we are locked out of the past.
          There is no going back into it
To retrieve what we've forgotten.

History is an idea whose time has come—
          And gone—

          And you—but no—you

Are never gone.
          A winter rain as black as bitterness
Gunshots the turrets, which swivel and gleam
          Under the glow of filaments.
People are shouting. A rifle goes off,
          And oh! I am as far away from you
But also as near

As a memory,
          As, for example, the memory of our knowledge
That we will die,
          Permanently. If human consciousness reaches outward
To include whatever it becomes conscious of, a destiny
          In the shape of a universe,
Infinite and bounded,

Then suffering must be absence
          Of memory, and even memory of pain
Is an argument for the existence of God.

I am trying to be precise
About this: not pain,
        Which is an argument for nothing,
Not even itself,

But memory of pain,
        The way we can choke, still, on remembered smoke
Rising from the camps, the way our minds go numb
        Remembering Siberia, how you fetaled yourself in the snow,
Your knees drawn up to your chest, your fists shoved into your groin
        For warmth, wanting only to go to sleep, and I kept trying
And trying to shake you awake *please God please.*

You had lined your shoes with newspaper,
        I could read the headlines through the holes,
And I was crying, and so angry with you
        For going away like that,
For falling carelessly out of consciousness
        Into that place as dark and dreamless
As Alzheimer's—

And thus, memory of pain
        Is an argument for the existence of
Everything, including you, the rain like a tapestry
        That moves, and the beautiful bird
Like a wound.

For even if it was someone else's past,
        Some other house,
Someone else's door that closed,
        Even if experience is private and nontransferable,
The experience is not the memory,
        Which may be shared, which is like bread to be shared
Among friends, which is like kindness and concern

For one another, the hand stretching across the table
        To offer a cup.

Remember *that*—

Understand *that*—

The smoke, the snow were not our horror,
        But the memory of horror has been handed us
And it is something we must take in.
        After the Holocaust, the two questions are,
Is poetry possible?
        And
What else is there?

But was it not obvious—it was not obvious—
        Why suffering would be the absence of memory. . . .
God, we said—this is the reason—is a presence
        Congruent with our consciousness of it, though also greater,
So that not to be conscious of God is to be out of grace.
        (Here, someone asks if a God that comes to know itself is not
Less than omniscient, therefore less than a God.)

The God that reveals itself
        As it comes to know itself
Possesses limitless knowledge, for the future does not exist
        Until that God exists,
An eternal God creating itself in time.

On the mountain, the light downrushing onto his face—

What is transfigured? Is it the one seen,
        Or the one seeing?
There was a moment when we knew ourselves

For who we were.
The roses were like red chalices
Filled with light,
And the sky was as clear as a declaration.

(Scarcely a cloud in sight—)

You remember, I know you remember,
This happened only yesterday,
All of it,
Before we woke to rain,
Blood, fire,
A new war—
A new poetry—